MIRACLE LIVING

Mary T Buckman
John F Campoli, I.V.Dei

First Printing -2015

Copyright ©, 2015 by Rev. John F. Campoli

Published by His Love Press
P.O. Box 1951, Brick, New Jersey 08723

Scripture Reference:
All Scripture quotations were taken from the HOLY BIBLE, NEW
INTERNATIONAL VERSION, copyright © 1973, 1978, 1984 by Inter-
national Bible Society.

ISBN-13:978-1512040135

Dedication

We dedicate this book to All the wonderful people we have met on ministry Most especially the people of Trinidad and Tobago. We had traveled to Trinidad to spread the Gospel of Jesus Christ and we received much more love and care than we could possibly imagine. Thank you all for allowing us to see Christ in you.

INTRODUCTION

Love prompted this book. Over the years we have met with thousands of people celebrating healing masses, days of recollection, weekend retreats and pilgrimages to faraway places. The questions and needs of those we have met are reflected in the book. We were aware that people have felt the love and touch of God in their life but they needed a way to build community, to make their faith grow and come alive. The result of this awareness is a book reinforcing the fact that God loves you as if you were the only person He ever made.

We are exposed to God's love by reading the Scripture, and then meditating on it, letting it touch both heart and mind. The questions at the end of each chapter are for personal reflection but also may serve as a discussion starter for a small group sharing which can make us aware that as a community of people we possess a collective wisdom, especially on the grass roots level. The group could be as small as two people. We all have a tendency to keep the wisdom to ourselves but after listening to the thoughts of others we are opened up to ideas that may never have crossed our minds before. God has a way of dealing with each person individually. He has touched each life in a unique way and sharing these moments helps us all grow in wisdom. There are no right or wrong answers, each person reading the questions is free to express what the Holy Spirit has placed in their heart. As Jean-Pierre de Caussade, in his book *Abandonment to Divine Providence* once wrote: *There is a universal Spirit which pervades every heart, speaking to each one individually. It speaks through Isaiah, Jeremiah, and Ezekiel. Without knowing it, all are instruments of that Spirit and all bring the message ever new to our world. And if souls knew how to unite themselves to that purpose their lives would be a succession of the Divine Scriptures, continuing to the end of time--not written on ink or on paper but on each human heart. Unlike the Holy Scriptures the Book of Life will not only be a history of the work of the Holy Spirit over the centuries written down every thought, word, deed and suffering of all souls. And that scripture will be a complete record of Divine Revelation. And so the sequel to the New Testament is being written now by action and suffering. Saintly souls are in succession of the prophets and the apostles, not by writing canonical books, by continuing the history of Divine purpose within their lives. Lives whose moments are so many syllables and sentences which is vividly expressed. The books of the Holy Spirit are living books. And every soul is involved in which the Divine Author makes a true revelation of His Word explaining it to every heart, unfolding it at every moment.*

The final part of each chapter is a Recipe for Miracle Living. Here, we commit to go forward living out what we have discovered. Being that living book of scripture we take that message of Christ into our daily lives, living it for all to see.

God bless you on your spiritual journey!

CONTENTS

Recipes
For
Miracle Living

1 Laughter

When the LORD brought back the captives to Zion, we were like men who dreamed.
Our mouths were filled with laughter, our tongues with songs of joy. Then it was said among the nations, "The LORD has done great things for them."
The LORD has done great things for us, and we are filled with joy.
Restore our fortunes, O LORD, like streams in the Negev.
Those who sow in tears will reap with songs of joy.
He who goes out weeping, carrying seed to sow, will return with songs of joy, carrying sheaves with him.

Psalm 126:1-6

Laughter is a precious gift from God for when we laugh we agree with God that all is good. Laughter knows no bounds. It has neither nationality, politics nor religion. It is the supreme equalizer. Even science, which can do many things, cannot teach us to laugh.

Laughter is infectious. When a person starts to laugh uncontrollably others seem to catch the same spirit. It releases the heaviness from our hearts and
leaves us feeling at peace. Joy is from God, a gift of the spirit. Dullness is from the devil who wants us to think that God does not care what happens in our life.
Someone once sent me a little formula for avoiding misery and allowing yourself to be open to God's gift of Laughter:

Choose to love – rather than hate
Choose to smile – rather than frown
Choose to build – rather than destroy
Choose to persevere – rather than quit

Choose to praise- rather than criticize
Choose to heal - rather than wound
Choose to give - rather than grasp

Even when things seem to be at their lowest ebb, try a little laughter. Remember Jesus told us that he came so that His joy would be ours and our joy may be complete.

Take Time for Reflection

Has the Lord ever led you out of captivity (health concerns, financial crisis, family problems, and emotional problems)?

Describe how you felt during the process.

Can you see how the Lord might have used the situation for an ultimate good? Explain

Thank the Lord in all things, realizing that even what might seem bad to me today, can be a source of rejoicing in the future because I know that "All things work for the good."

2 Fasting and Feasting

Why have we fasted,' they say, 'and you have not seen it? Why have we humbled ourselves, and you have not noticed?' "Yet on the day of your fasting, you do as you please and exploit all your workers. Your fasting ends in quarreling and strife, and in striking each other with wicked fists. You cannot fast as you do today and expect your voice to be heard on high. Is this the kind of fast I have chosen, only a day for a man to humble himself? Is it only for bowing one's head like a reed and for lying on sackcloth and ashes? Is that what you call a fast, a day acceptable to the LORD? "Is not this the kind of fasting I have chosen: to loose the chains of injustice and untie the cords of the yoke, to set the oppressed free and break every yoke? Is it not to share your food with the hungry and to provide the poor wanderer with shelter-- when you see the naked, to clothe him, and not to turn away from your own flesh and blood? Then your light will break forth like the dawn, and your healing will quickly appear; then your righteousness will go before you, and the glory of the LORD will be your rear guard. Then you will call, and the LORD will answer; you will cry for help, and he will say: Here am I. "If you do away with the yoke of oppression, with the pointing finger and malicious talk, and if you spend yourselves in behalf of the hungry and satisfy the needs of the oppressed, then your light will rise in the darkness, and your night will become like the noonday. The LORD will guide you always; he will satisfy your needs in a sun-scorched land and will strengthen your frame. You will be like a well-watered garden, like a spring whose waters never fail. Isa 58:3-11

Fast from judging others; feast on the Spirit dwelling within them.
Fast from emphasizing differences, feast on the unity of all.
Fast from thoughts of illness, feast on God's healing power.
Fast from criticism, feast on the positive attributes of others.
Fast from putting others down, feast on blessing them.
Fast from complaining, feast on appreciation for the gifts God gives you.
Fast from pessimism, feast on optimism.
Fast from anger, feast on peace.
Fast from worry, feast on divine order.
Fast from discontent, feast on gratitude.
Fast from negative thinking, feast on developing positive attitudes.
Fast from bitterness, feast on forgiveness.
Fast from self-concern, feast on compassion for others.
Fast from discouragement, feast on hope.
Fast from fear, feast on trust in God's love for you.
Fast from ideas that depress, feast on God's promises that inspire.
Fast from idle gossip, feast on purposeful silence.
Fast from problems that overwhelm, feast on supporting prayer.
Fast from the shadows of sorrow, feast on the feast on the sunlight of peace.
Fast each day from rethinking the hurtful things that you have done or from the hurtful things that others have done to you. Ask God to gift you with a new way to think.

ʳ Reflection:

; affect others more than yourself? (Are you a "less
n you are hungry?)

How can fasting make you a better person?

While you are fasting, what are you feasting on?

What did you do for Lent? Were you successful?

Feast on being merciful to others, while fasting from anything negative in your life. Feast each day on all that is positive and you will never need to fear tomorrow or regret the past.

3 A Love Story

I pray that out of his glorious riches he may strengthen
you with power through his Spirit in your inner being,
so that Christ may dwell in your hearts through faith.
And I pray that you, being rooted and established in
love, may have power, together with all the saints, to
grasp how wide and long and high and deep is the love
of Christ,   and to know this love that surpasses
knowledge-- that you may be filled to the measure of all
the fullness of God.   Now to him who is able to do
immeasurably more than all we ask or imagine,
according to his power that is at work within us, to him
be glory in the church and in Christ Jesus throughout
all generations, forever and ever! Amen.

Ephesians 3:16-21

One day, I woke early in the morning to watch the sunrise. Ah the
beauty of God's creation is beyond description. As I watched, I
praised God for His beautiful work. As I sat there, I felt the Lord's
presence with me.

He asked me, "Do you love me?"

I answered, "Of course, God! You are my Lord and Savior!"

Then He asked, "If you were physically handicapped, would
you still love me?"

I was perplexed. I looked down upon my arms, legs and the rest of my
body and wondered how many things I wouldn't be able to do-the
things that I took for granted. And I answered, "It would be tough

Lord, but I would still love you."

Then the Lord said, "If you were blind, would you still love my creation?"

How could I love something without being able to see it? Then I thought of all the blind people in the world and how many of them still loved God and His creation. So I answered, "It's hard to think of it, but I would still love you."

The Lord then asked me, "If you were deaf, would you still listen to my word?"

How could I listen to anything being deaf? Then I understood. Listening to God's Word is not merely using our ears, but our hearts. I answered, "It would be tough, but I would still listen to your word."

The Lord then asked, "If you were mute, would you still praise My Name?"

How could I praise without a voice? Then it occurred to me: God wants us to sing from our very heart and soul. It never matters what we sound like. And praising God is not always with a song, but when we are persecuted, we give God praise with our words of thanks. So I answered, "Though I could not physically sing, I would still praise Your Name.

And the Lord asked, "Do you really love me?"

With courage and a strong conviction, I answered boldly, "Yes Lord! I love you because you are the one and true God!" I thought I had answered well, but... God asked,

"THEN WHY DO YOU SIN?"

I answered, "Because I am only human. I am not perfect."

"THEN WHY IN TIMES OF PEACE DO YOU STRAY THE FURTHEST?"

WHY ONLY IN TIMES OF TROUBLE DO YOU PRAY THE EARNEST?"

No answers, only tears.

The Lord continued: "Why only sing at fellowships and retreats? Why seek me only in times of worship? Why ask things so selfishly? Why ask things so unfaithfully?"

The tears continued to roll down my cheeks.

"Why are you ashamed of me? Why are you not spreading the good news? Why in times of persecution, you cry to others when I offer my shoulder to cry on? Why make excuses when I give you opportunities to serve in My Name?"

I tried to answer, but there was no answer to give.

"You are blessed with life. I made you not to throw this gift away. I have blessed you with talents to serve me, but you continue to turn away. I have revealed My Word to you, but you do not gain in knowledge. I have spoken to you but your ears were closed. I have shown My blessings to you, but your eyes were turned away. I have sent you servants, but you sat idly by as they were pushed away. I have heard your prayers and I have answered them all." DO YOU TRULY LOVE ME?"

I could not answer. How could I? I was embarrassed beyond belief. I had no excuse. What could I say to this? When my heart had cried out and the tears had flowed, I said, "Please forgive me Lord. I am unworthy to be your child."

The Lord answered, "That is My Grace, My child."

I asked, "Then why do you continue to forgive me? Why do you love me so?"

The Lord answered, "Because you are my creation. You are my child. I will never abandon you. When you cry, I will have compassion and cry with you. When you shout with joy, I will laugh with you. When you are down, I will encourage you. When you fall, I will raise you up. When you are tired, I will carry you. I will be with you till the end of days, and I will love you forever."

Never had I cried so hard before. How could I have been so cold? How could I have hurt God as I had done? I asked God, "How much do you love me?"

The Lord stretched out His arms, and I saw His nail-pierced hands. I bowed down at the feet of Christ, my Savior. And for the first time, I truly prayed.

(Author Unknown.)

Take Time for Reflection

What do you think happens when Christ dwells in your heart?
What is the power that the Spirit brings?
What do you think Paul means when he says that love surpasses all
knowledge?

**Think often of the love that God has for you. The love
witch was revealed in the death and resurrection of
Jesus. For God so loved you that he gave his only Son .
. .**

4 Seek and you shall find

"Ask and it will be given to you; seek and you will find; knock and the door will be opened to you. For everyone who asks receives; he who seeks finds and to him who knocks the door will be opened."

Matthew 7:7-9

On one of my first trips to Betania I had a very interesting experience. On the eve of the anniversary many people were gathered by the Grotto of Our Lady of Betania and praying. All of a sudden a wind came up and many of us felt like it was raining and yet we weren't getting wet. Then, all of a sudden in the midst of the crowd there stood a woman who was covered in gold dust. It was amazing to see. Everyone gathered around her, the excitement of seeing this was very overwhelming. It was so amazing. I remember many people were firing questions at her. Where are you from? She answered Florida. Why did this happen to you? So many were reaching to touch her and she remained so calm. Then one person said to her, "My God you are so blessed!" She answered calmly, "Yes, I always am."

I have to tell you I was amazed at her answer. I put myself in her place and pretended that I was covered in gold dust, trying to see how I would react in such a situation. I laughed at how I would react so differently than she did. I probably would have been jumping around asking for a mirror so that I could see myself. I probably would have been so excited I could not have contained the feeling. I know that I would not have calmly responded "Yes, I always am." I guess I would have reacted so crazily that Our Lady knew not to cover me with gold dust!

I thought about this often after I returned home. I spoke about it to a priest and he said that he was not surprised at her reaction. She expected to be touched and she was. He said that when we go forward in faith God meets us. True faith believes that prayers will move mountains…Next time you pray for rain, carry an umbrella.

Take Time for Reflection

Meditating on this Scripture, what comes to your mind?

How do you explain it when you have prayed for things and don't feel that your prayers have been answered?

What do you think God is saying when He tells us to do this?

What are you seeking? What should you be seeking?

I will make an effort to see the hand of God in my life. I am not going to spend time worrying about the past, the things that cannot be changed or worrying about the future, but I will make an effort to live not in the day but in the present moment. He is in the present moment that is why it is a "present".

5 Reacting With Love

Because of the increase of wickedness, the love of most will grow cold, but he who stands firm to the end will be saved.

Matthew 24:12-14

Margaret was in great need of a winter coat. She had been living on a very tight budget. Then she noticed a newspaper advertisement. Her local department store would be having a sale on coats. She was very excited. She had been wearing a worn out coat all winter and was waiting for the end of the year sale. Finally, it was happening.

She arrived at the store and began to try on coats one after the other. Nothing was fitting. Then all of a sudden there was "The Coat". She checked the price and it was perfect. She brought it over to the checkout counter and waited at the end of a long line. Finally, it was her turn and the saleswoman took the coat and rung up the price. Margaret took out her checkbook and wrote the check. All of a sudden she realized that she had switched pocketbooks and had left her identification in the other bag. She had nothing to give the woman to verify her address. The salesperson told her that she could not accept the check without proper identification. Margaret asked her if she could hold onto the coat until she returned but she was informed that that was not allowed for the sale items, since it was a special one day sale. Down hearted, Margaret reached for the coat, offering to take it to the rack and saying a prayer that no one would buy it in her absence. All of a sudden it became apparent to her that the man in line behind her was very impatient. He was muttering and reaching for his wallet. The next minute he was flashing his money and telling the salesperson, "I want that coat. I have the money give it to me now." The salesperson was obviously aggravated with him but could do nothing short of handing him the coat. She looked apologetically at Margaret.

The other people on the line looked at him disgustedly too, they couldn't believe that he would be so unfeeling.

Margaret left the counter and was making her way out of the store, feeling so sad. Back at the counter the man was telling the salesperson to hurry up, forget the bag just give him the coat. He took it and then made a mad dash for the exit. He caught up with Margaret, and placed the coat around her shoulders. He said, "I saw what happened back in the store. I wanted you to have the coat – take it and have a wonderful day. Maybe sometime when you are wearing it you will remember to say a prayer for me." Then he gave her a wink and went off, waving. Needless to say, Margaret was shocked. Never has a coat meant more to her. It is these acts of kindness that make Christ real in the world. May you be blessed with such a happening in your life and may you be an instrument of kindness in someone else's life.

Take Time for Reflection

We live in very polarized times, we see so much good and so much evil. Often one begets the other. Recently, how did you react when someone hurt you?

Have you observed someone reacting kindly to someone who was cruel to them? How did that make you feel?

How do you feel inside when you react mean to someone who is aggressive?

How do you feel when you act kind to someone's aggression?

I will focus on God and I will take the different unkind things that happen in my day and react to that as I think Jesus would. I will keep in mind the initials "WWJD" "What would Jesus Do" as I handle different situations.

6 Discouragement

For this reason, since the day we heard about you, we have not stopped praying for you and asking God to fill you with the knowledge of his will through all spiritual wisdom and understanding. And we pray this in order that you may live a life worthy of the Lord and may please him in every way: bearing fruit in every good work, growing in the knowledge of God, being strengthened with all power according to his glorious might so that you may have great endurance and patience, and joyfully giving thanks to the Father, who has qualified you to share in the inheritance of the saints in the kingdom of light. For he has rescued us from the dominion of darkness and brought us into the kingdom of the Son he loves, in whom we have redemption, the forgiveness of sins. He is the image of the invisible God, the firstborn over all creation. For by him all things were created: things in heaven and on earth, visible and invisible, whether thrones or powers or rulers or authorities; all things were created by him and for him. He is before all things, and in him all things hold together. And he is the head of the body, the church; he is the beginning and the firstborn from among the dead, so that in everything he might have the supremacy. For God was pleased to have all his fullness dwell in him, and through him to reconcile to himself all things, whether things on earth or things in heaven, by making peace through his blood, shed on the cross.

Colossians 1:9-20

I once heard a story of a man who was lost in the woods. After wandering for days in the dark overgrown forest, he came upon a great red barn in the middle of a clearing. Seeking refuge from the howling wind of a storm that seemed to rage perpetually in the forest, he took refuge in the barn. Once inside, he noticed that the barn was filled with bins of seed. Looking at the labels on the bins he saw such names as anger, rage, fear, lust, greed, immorality and every other type of sin or dark emotion. Then, to his astonishment, he realized that this was the barn where Satan kept his supply of seed to be sown into human hearts. More curious than fearful, he began to explore the piles and bins of seeds around him. He couldn't help but notice that the containers labeled 'seeds of discouragement' far outnumbered any other type of seed.

Just as the man had drawn this conclusion, one of Satan's foremost demons arrived to pick up a fresh supply of seed. The man asked him why there was such an abundance of discouragement seeds. The demon laughed, "because they are so effective and they take root so quickly.' The man then asked if the seeds of discouragement grow everywhere. At this the demon became sullen. He glared at the man and admitted in disgust, "No. They never seem to thrive in the heart of a grateful person."

Be thankful for what you have, today. And trust the Lord to take supply of what you don't have.

Take Time for Reflection

What is a *life worthy of the Lord?*

What should be the fruit of our work? How do we judge the fruit? (See Galatians 5)

Paul talks about being strengthened to have endurance. What means do you have at your disposal for this strengthening? What things can help keep you from being discouraged?

I will work on developing a grateful heart to help keep me from being discouraged. I will start to thank God for the things I have been taking for granted. Think how many morning I get out of bed and don't even say "Thank You". Many people in this world do not even have a bed to get out of, I will think to say "Thank You" when I get dressed, how many people have to sleep and then wear the same clothes, I will say "Thank You" when I was up...so many do not have a place to do that. Yes, I will begin to be very grateful.

7 Real Victory

> If God is for us, who can be against us? He who did not spare his own Son, but gave him up for us all--how will he not also, along with him, graciously give us all things? Who will bring any charge against those whom God has chosen? It is God who justifies. Who is he that condemns? Christ Jesus, who died--more than that, who was raised to life--is at the right hand of God and is also interceding for us. Who shall separate us from the love of Christ? Shall trouble or hardship or persecution or famine or nakedness or danger or sword? As it is written: "For your sake we face death all day long; we are considered as sheep to be slaughtered." No, in all these things we are more than conquerors through him who loved us. For I am convinced that neither death nor life, neither angels nor demons, neither the present nor the future, nor any powers,
>   neither height nor depth, nor anything else in all creation, will be able to separate us from the love of God that is in Christ Jesus our Lord. Romans 8:31-39

Recently, a friend sent me this story. I think that if we were to allow the transformation that takes place in the woman in the story to happen in our lives, we would really know the meaning of Paul's words that "we are more than conquerors" in Christ Jesus.

The park bench was deserted as I sat down to read beneath the long, straggly branches of an old willow tree. Disillusioned by life with good reason to frown for the world was intent on dragging me down.

And if that weren't enough to ruin my day, a young boy out of breath approached me, all tired from play. He stood right before me with his head tilted down and said with great excitement, "Look what I found!"

In his hand was a flower, and what a pitiful sight, with its petals all worn - not enough rain, or too little light. Wanting him to take his dead flower and go off to play, I faked a small smile and then shifted away.

But instead of retreating he sat next to my side and placed the flower to his nose and declared with overacted surprise, "It sure smells pretty and it's beautiful, too. That's why I picked it; here, it's for you."

The weed before me was dying or dead. Not vibrant of colors: orange, yellow or red. But I knew I must take it, or he might never leave. So I reached for the flower, and replied, "Just what I need."

But instead of him placing the flower in my hand, He held it midair without reason or plan. It was then that I noticed for the very first time that weed-toting boy could not see: he was blind.

I heard my voice quiver: tears shone in the sun as I thanked him for picking the very best one. You're welcome," he smiled, and then ran off to play, Unaware of the impact he'd had on my day.

I sat there and wondered how he managed to see a self-pitying woman beneath an old willow tree. How did he know of my self-indulged plight? Perhaps from his heart, he'd been blessed with true sight.

Through the eyes of a blind child at last I could see, the problem was not with the world; the problem was with me. And for all of those times I myself had been blind, I vowed to see the beauty in life, and appreciate every second that's mine.

And then I held that wilted flower up to my nose and breathed in the fragrance of a beautiful rose and smiled as I watched that young boy, another weed in his hand, about to change the life of another old man.

Take Time for Reflection

If God is for us, how do we react when the world seems to be against us?

Paul reminds us that we have the victory in Christ, yet joy is not always present. What are the things that rob you of joy?

Do you ever feel that God is not "for you?" How do you deal with these feelings?

I will shift my focus from myself to others. I will take a positive attitude refusing to feel sorry for myself, realizing that in Jesus I have everything I need.

8 The Better Part

As Jesus and his disciples were on their way, he came to
a village where a woman named Martha opened her
home to him. She had a sister called Mary, who sat at
the Lord's feet listening to what he said. But Martha
was distracted by all the preparations that had to be
made. She came to him and asked, "Lord, don't you
care that my sister has left me to do the work by
myself? Tell her to help me!" "Martha, Martha," the
Lord answered, "you are worried and upset about many
things, but only one thing is needed. Mary has chosen
what is better, and it will not be taken away from her."

Luke 10:38-42

One day this expert was speaking to a group of business students and,
to drive home a point, used an illustration I'm sure those students will
never forget. After I share it with you, you will never forget it either.

As he stood in front of the group of high-powered over achievers, he
said, "Okay, time for a quiz." He pulled out a one-gallon, wide-
mouthed Mason jar and set it on a table in front of him. Then he
produced about a dozen fist-sized rocks and carefully placed them, one
at a time, into the jar.

When the jar was filled to the top and no more rocks would fit inside,
he asked, "Is this jar full?" Everyone in the class said, "Yes."

Then he said, "Really?" He reached under the table and pulled out a
bucket of gravel. Then he dumped some gravel in and shook the jar
causing pieces of gravel to work themselves down into the spaces
between the big rocks.

Then he smiled and asked the group once more, "Is the jar full?" By this time the class was onto him. "Probably not," one of them answered. "Good!" he replied. And he reached under the table and brought out a bucket of sand. He started dumping the sand in and it went into the space between the rocks and the gravel. Once more he asked the question, "Is this jar full?" "No!" the class shouted.

Once again he said, "Good!" Then he grabbed a pitcher of water and began to pour it in until the jar was filled to the brim. Then he looked up at the class and asked, "What is the point of this illustration?"

One eager beaver raised his hand and said, "The point is, no matter how full your schedule is, if you try really hard, you can always fit some more things into it!"

Take Time for Reflection

If God is for us, how do we react when the world seems to be against us?

Paul reminds us that we have the victory in Christ, yet joy is not always present. What are the things that rob you of joy?

Do you ever feel that God is not "for you?" How do you deal with these feelings?

I will shift my focus from myself to others. I will take a positive attitude refusing to feel sorry for myself, realizing that in Jesus I have everything I need.

9 Listen

My dear brothers, take note of this: Everyone should be quick to listen, slow to speak and slow to become angry, for man's anger does not bring about the righteous life that God desires. Therefore, get rid of all moral filth and the evil that is so prevalent and humbly accept the word planted in you, which can save you. Do not merely listen to the word, and so deceive yourselves. Do what it says. Anyone who listens to the word but does not do what it says is like a man who looks at his face in a mirror and, after looking at himself, goes away and immediately forgets what he looks like. But the man who looks intently into the perfect law that gives freedom, and continues to do this, not forgetting what he has heard, but doing it-- he will be blessed in what he does. If anyone considers himself religious and yet does not keep a tight rein on his tongue, he deceives himself and his religion is worthless.

James 1:19-26

Listening is always a difficult thing for us. We don't even like to listen to God. So often we feel that we have all the answers.

Listening to others is even more difficult. We like to play God in their lives – dishing out great helpings of our advice. Most of the time all another person wants of us is a willing ear. When we allow another person to talk out their problems, we are really providing the space for them to "hear" God speaking the answers in their heart. A long time ago, someone gave me this poem on listening.

When I ask you to listen to me and you start giving advice, you have not done what I asked.

*When I ask you to listen to me and you begin to tell me why I shouldn't
feel that way, you are trampling on my feelings.*
*When I ask you to listen to me and you feel you have to do something to
solve my problem, you have failed me, strange as that may seem.*
Listen! All I ask is that you listen, not talk, or do --- just hear me.
*Advice is cheap. 50 cents will get you both Dear Abby and Anne Landers
in the same newspaper.*
*And I can do for myself; I'm not helpless. Maybe discouraged and
faltering, but not helpless.*
*When you do something for me that I can and need to do for myself, you
contribute to my fear and weakness. But, when you accept as a simple fact that I do
feel what I feel, no matter how irrational, then I can quit trying to convince you and
get about the business of understanding what's behind this irrational feeling.*
*And when that's clear, the answers are obvious and I don't need advice.
Irrational feelings make sense when we understand what's behind them. So, please
listen and lust hear me.*
And, if you want to talk, wait a minute for your turn; and I'll listen to you.

Anonymous

We need to respect others. Accept their worth and value. Never let our
"good advice" stand in the way of their listening to the voice of God
speaking to them.

Take time for Reflection

Prayer is talking with God. Part of talking with another involves listening. How much time do you spend listening to God? In what ways do you listen to God?

Do you find that you already have decided the answers God should give to your prayers? Do you act on His answers or on your own? When God puts something on your heart how do you act on it?

James tells us to be "quick to listen, slow to speak." How much time do you spend listening to others? Do you respect their opinions or try to be the fix-it person trying to get others to do your will?

I will concentrate on listening both to God and to others without interruption, comments or pre-conceived ideas. I will make an effort to not only speak to God and tell Him what is happening in my life, but I will then sit quiet and listen for Him to speak to my heart.

10 You have got to be Kidding

Then the Lord answered Job out of the storm. He said:
Who is this that darkens my counsel with words without knowledge?
Brace yourself like a man: I will question you, and you shall answer me.
Where were you when I laid the earth's foundation?
Tell me if you understand.
Who marked off its dimensions? Surely you know!
Who stretched a measuring line across it?
On what were its footings set, or who laid its cornerstone—while the morning stars sang together and all the angels shouted for joy?
Who shut up the sea behind doors …
Have you ever given orders to the morning or shown the dawn its place?…
Have you comprehended the vast expanses of the earth? Tell me, if you know all this.

Job 38:1-8a, 12, 18

Everyone was very excited to hear the report of the Social Concerns Committee so when Fr. Jack called on Bill to give his account a hush fell over the room. Bill cleared his throat and took everyone by surprise when He announced: "I have some very discouraging, no, maybe aggravating news. To refresh our memory or to fill in the new members with what has been happening I will open by saying that most of my comments tonight will concern the Smith file. The Smiths have been a member of our parish for 10 years. They had suffered quite a set back a few years ago. Mrs. Smith, the mother of four young children had passed away after a long illness. Shortly after Mrs. Smith's death the house had suffered damage from a fire that began in the basement. Different members of the parish who had visited the Smith home reported that things were bad there and only getting worse. No matter how Mr. Smith tried, he was having difficulty keeping a job, raising the children and now trying to make repairs on the house. Then the parish inherited a home. We on the Parish Council voted to use this property along with our talents to help out the Smiths. With great excitement we took on this project. Repairs were made on the house along with a decision to paint every room in the house white. We had all felt that since we were unaware of the furnishings and taste of the Smith family we would be unable to pick out colored paint for the different rooms. The reason I am mentioning all this is to say that before tonight's meeting I visited the Smith family. I went to ask them how things were going and all I heard from Mr. Smith was that he was so sick of the white rooms…"white, white, white, he complained, I am so sick of looking at white walls." I must admit, said Bill, I am angry and disgusted at Mr. Smith".

Margaret, head of the Liturgy Committee said, "Bill, you have to be kidding. I can't believe that was Mr. Smith's comments. That takes a lot of nerve."

The whole room began to murmur. Then all of a sudden, Fr. Jack spoke up. "Before this goes any further and before any one picks up the first stone I would like to make a few remarks. Bill, while I was listening to your report I was struck with this thought: I wonder if God is having the same reaction to us when we turn to him with our complaints and our grumbling about this and that. Maybe God thinks…they have to be kidding. Look at them, look where they live, how blessed they are in so many ways. I can't believe that they are still complaining. Do they notice the sky, the stars at night sky, the flowers, the rivers, the sea, the trees, the birds, the animals? I wonder if they would ever be satisfied. I admit what happened with the Smith family is annoying but maybe we too, with our pleadings to God are also annoying. Maybe we all have to think a little more. Mr. Smith wasn't any guiltier than we are. He, like us probably didn't even realize what he was saying. I am sure if he took time to think he would have been grateful for all we did. He just got into being negative. I suggest that we take this as a lesson. Let's make it a point to look at our blessings and spend more time thanking God and less time begging for more.

Let's stop taking things for granted. You, know I think we learned a great lesson tonight".

Take Time for Reflection

How many times do we think we know better than God what should happen in our life?
God speaks to Job and forces him to admit that he does not know everything.

Looking back over our lives what is an outstanding time that certainly showed that God's ways are not our ways?

In hindsight what good did you see that came out of that instance?

When is the last time I took a good look at nature and saw the wonder of God?

I will make it a point to notice my blessings. I will put aside the complaints I have and focus on what God has already given to me. I will make it a point to be thankful.

11 Jesus is My Pilot

Praise be to the God and Father of our Lord Jesus Christ, who has blessed us in the heavenly realms with every spiritual blessing in Christ. For he chose us in him before the creation of the world to be holy and blameless in his sight. In love he predestined us to be adopted as his sons through Jesus Christ, in accordance with his pleasure and will---to the praise of his glorious grace, which he has freely given us in the one he loves. In him we have redemption through his blood, the forgiveness of sins, in accordance with the riches of God's grace that he lavished on us with all wisdom and understanding. He made known to us the mystery of his will according to his good pleasure, which he purposed in Christ to be put into effect when the times will have reached their fulfillment—to bring all things in heaven and on earth together under one head, Christ.

Ephesians 1:3-10

Quite a while ago I heard a story:

Jesus and I decided to take a tandem bike ride one sunny afternoon. I jumped on the front of the bike and off we went. I felt quite secure knowing that he was on the back seat. Certainly nothing bad could happen when I had God right behind me. We peddled on and on, riding here and there, looking at this and that. It was a very enjoyable time, but as the day wore on it seemed to get almost tedious, even a little boring. I was getting ready to suggest that we turn around and head for home when Jesus tapped me on the shoulder and asked if I would let him get in the front and take over the steering. Well, I was getting a little bored with it all so it seemed like a great idea. We switched seats. Jesus began to peddle and we started flying over the paths and roadways. Off we zoomed this way and that way; I couldn't seem to control anything. One minute I was going around this curve, the next minute I was racing downhill, almost pell-mell. I kept tapping Him on the back and suggesting that we slow down or even stop but He would just laugh and say, "Don't worry, learn to trust me" and we would fly off in another direction. Well, I can say that the afternoon was certainly not tedious and not boring. It was a breathtaking, exhilarating day. I saw more things, and experienced more than I had ever before. I realized that when God is the pilot things happen…life happens.

What a day! I would beg Him to slow down or to stop and He would have to remind me to trust. He is God and He loves me so much, yet I didn't want him to steer or to be the pilot. I was afraid to take a risk. What could I have been thinking?

Take Time for Reflection:

God has loved us and chosen us in Christ, from the beginning. Try to comprehend that.

What thoughts come to your mind?

God has given us freedom and asks us to give him filial response...He knows it is difficult. We must die to ourselves. What scares us with that?

He makes known to us the mystery of His will—to bring all things in heaven and on earth together under one head...that is God's will. What is it in our life that causes us division?

What do you think would be a "baby step" that you could do in letting go and letting God?

I will take it one day at a time, trying my best to let go of the things that I hold onto and use my gifts and talents to be loving and caring of those that God has put in my path. When I see a person I will not hold on to petty slights but reach out trying to spread the love of God.

12 Last Chance

No one knows about that day or hour, not even the angels in heaven, nor the Son, but only the Father. As it was in the days of Noah, so it will be at the coming of the Son of Man, for in the days before the flood, people were eating and drinking, marrying and giving in marriage, up to the day Noah entered the ark; and they knew nothing about what would happen until the flood came and took them all away. That is how it will be at the coming of the son of Man. Two men will be in the field; one will be taken and the other left. Two women will be grinding with a hand mill; one will be taken and the other left. Therefore keep watch, because you do not know on what day your Lord will come.

Mt 24:36-43

You've heard...Live each day as if it was your last, take that idea one step further...treat other people as if it was their last day!

Can you imagine the difference that would make? How different would you treat someone if you knew that you would not have the opportunity to ever be with that person again? Think of the last person that you saw. Would you have behaved differently toward them if you thought you would never see them again? Petty moods and distractions would have not taken up so much time. We probably would have really paid attention to what they were saying...really gave them quality time. Pleasant things which we let slip by would take on the importance they deserve and many a so-called "crisis" would seem so insignificant. It would be amazing how kind we would be if you felt that they would not be there tomorrow.

Once, I traveled with a friend to a hospital in Boston, Massachusetts. She was an outpatient so we stayed at a hotel near the hospital. The waiter was very kind and friendly and on the last day of our visit he sat down and had a very enlightening conversation with us. He told us that since he began working in this restaurant his life had changed. He said that because of the proximity to the hospital many people came there when visiting a sick family member or friend. Time after time, they would share with him their story. Listening to the different customers, he began to learn how quickly life changes. Over and over, he heard stories of lives being altered without warning. He said he began to appreciate all the people in his life. His family took on the importance they deserved and then he said it went beyond that. He started to treat every person he met as kindly as he could. He said he never wanted to look back and regret sharp words said to another. He became aware that because of an accident he could be left without an opportunity to ever take them back. He said he learned to treat each person he met as if he would never have the opportunity to be with them again. Then he smiled and said, "And you know what happened after I had this attitude. I wound up with so many more friends and so much happier than I have ever been in my life."

For myself, it was great meeting him. I think I met one of the wisest men I will ever meet.

Treating people in our life as if we would never have a second chance would make us much more loving. There are so many missed opportunities because we are not living in the present with the people we love. Make every moment count. We might not have a second chance.

"For the few years we still have to live in this world, we must do our best to spend our time as well as possible." St. Bernadette

Take Time for Reflection:

Keep watch for you do not know what day the Lord will come. When you think about this statement, what do you think that you personally should watch out for in your own life?

Picture Jesus standing in the back of the room...you turn around and you see Him and he is pointing at you and beckoning for you to come...what would your reaction be?

Who was the last person you spent time with and how was the time spent? Was it quality or quantity?

If you knew that this was the day of Jesus' Second Coming would you change what you planned on doing?

I will make an effort to live my life as if Jesus was coming at any moment to call me home. I will not put off forgiving a friend or delaying a kindness. I will make a special effort to be and do what Jesus would want me in every situation.

13 Something Better

When I came to you, brothers, I did not come with eloquence or superior wisdom as I proclaimed to you the testimony about God.   For I resolved to know nothing while I was with you except Jesus Christ and him crucified. I came to you in weakness and fear, and with much trembling. My message and my preaching were not with wise and persuasive words, but with a demonstration of the Spirit's power, so that your faith might not rest on men's wisdom, but on God's power. We do, however, speak a message of wisdom among the mature, but not the wisdom of this age or of the rulers of this age, who are coming to nothing. No, we speak of God's secret wisdom, a wisdom that has been hidden and that God destined for our glory before time began. None of the rulers of this age understood it, for if they had, they would not have crucified the Lord of
    However, as it is written: "No eye has seen, no ear has heard, no mind has conceived what God has prepared for those who love him"-- but God has revealed it to us by his Spirit. The Spirit searches all things, even the deep things of God.

1 Corinthians 2:1-10

There was a woman who had been diagnosed with cancer and had been given 3 months to live.   Her doctor told her to start making preparations to die (something we all should be doing all of the time.)

She contacted her pastor and had him come to her house to discuss certain aspects of her final wishes.   She told him which songs she wanted sung at the service, what scriptures she would like read, and what she wanted to be wearing.   The woman also told her pastor that she wanted to be buried with her favorite bible.

Everything was in order and the pastor was preparing to leave when the woman suddenly remembered something very important to her. "There's one more thing." She said excitedly. "What's that?" came the pastor's reply."

"This is very important." The woman continued. "I want to be buried with a fork in my right hand."

The pastor stood looking at the woman not knowing quite what to say. "That shocks you doesn't it?" The woman asked.

"Well to be honest, I'm puzzled by the request," said the pastor.

The woman explained. "In all my years of attending church socials and functions where food was involved (and let's be honest, food is an important part of any church event; spiritual or otherwise); my favorite part was when whoever was clearing away the dishes of the main course would lean over and say 'you can keep your fork.' It was my favorite part because I knew that something better was coming. When they told me to keep my fork I knew that something great was about to be given to me. It wasn't Jell-O or pudding. It was cake or pie. Something with substance. So I just want people to see me there in that casket with a fork in my hand and I want them to wonder 'What's with the fork?' Then I want you to tell them: 'Something better is coming so keep your fork too.'"

The pastor's eyes were welled up with tears of joy as he hugged the woman goodbye. He knew this would be one of the last times he would see her before her death. But he also knew that that woman had a better grasp of heaven than he did. She KNEW that something better was coming.

At the funeral people were walking by the woman's casket and they saw the pretty dress she was wearing and her favorite bible and the fork placed in her right hand. Over and over the pastor heard the question "What's with the fork?" And over and over he smiled.

During his message the pastor told the people of the conversation he had with the woman shortly before she died. He also told them about the fork and about what it symbolized to her. The pastor told the people how he could not stop thinking about the fork and told them that they probably would not be able to stop thinking about it either. He was right.

So the next time you reach down for your fork, let it remind you oh so gently that there is something better coming.

Take Time for Reflection

How is the Spirit's power demonstrated in your life? Give some examples of things that you see as a basis for your faith.

What parts of Jesus' message do you think people have a difficult time accepting?

What is your idea of the things "God has prepared for those who love him"?

Instead of allowing my burdens to overwhelm me, I will focus on the fact that God has something better in store—as long as I keep on being loving.

14 He is Always Here

But now, this is what the LORD says-- he who created you, O Jacob, he who formed you, O Israel: "Fear not, for I have redeemed you; I have called you by name; you are mine. When you pass through the waters, I will be with you; and when you pass through the rivers, they will not sweep over you. When you walk through the fire, you will not be burned; the flames will not set you ablaze. For I am the LORD, your God, the Holy One of Israel, your Savior; I give Egypt for your ransom, Cush and Seba in your stead. Since you are precious and honored in my sight, and because I love you, I will give men in exchange for you, and people in exchange for your life. Do not be afraid, for I am with you; I will bring your children from the east and gather you from the west. I will say to the north, 'Give them up!' and to the south, 'Do not hold them back.' Bring my sons from afar and my daughters from the ends of the earth--everyone who is called by my name, whom I created for my glory, whom I formed and made."

Isaiah 43:1-7

Sometimes it's difficult for us to feel the presence and action of God in our lives. We look for him, but often can't find him. I think that part of the problem is that we look for him in the wrong places.

God made you—you are his. He will always reveal his presence if you look in the right places. I think the following poem says it well:

God, Are You Real?"

The child whispered, "God, speak to me"
And a meadowlark sang.
The child did not hear.
So the child yelled, "God, speak to me!"
And the thunder rolled across the sky
But the child did not listen.

The child looked around and said,
"God let me see you" and a star shone brightly
But the child did not notice
And the child shouted,
"God show me a miracle!"
And a life was born but the child did not know.
So the child cried out in despair,
"Touch me God, and let me know you are here!"

Whereupon God reached down
And touched the child.
But the child brushed the butterfly away
And walked away unknowingly.

Author Unknown

Take Time for Reflection

Give some examples of how God has been present in your life.

Have there been times when it seems that God has not been present in your life? Describe these times.

The Lord tells us not to be afraid. Why do you think so many people get overwhelmed with fear? How can we overcome the fear?

I will focus on seeing the presence of God in everything and everyone.

15 When the Saints Go Marching In

Therefore, since we are surrounded by such a great cloud of witnesses, let us throw off everything that hinders and the sin that so easily entangles, and let us run with perseverance the race marked out for us. Let us fix our eyes on Jesus, the author and perfector of our faith, who for the joy set before him endured the cross, scorning its shame, and sat down at the right hand of the throne of God. Consider him who endured such opposition from sinful men, so that you will not grow weary and lose heart.

Hebrews 12:1-3

We are all called to be saints. And what's holiness? Walking around with our hands folded? Being on our knees all the time? Fasting? Abstaining? Saying five rosaries a day? Spending ten hours before the Blessed Sacrament? No. None of that is holiness. It may be expressions of a person's piety but they're not holiness.

Some people think that holiness is being an angel. But this can't be holiness, because if God wanted you to be an angel He would have put you on a cloud and given you a harp. He didn't do that. He planted your feet here on earth.

About four years ago I was giving a talk on holiness at St. Francis church in Bend, Oregon. It was at the 11 o'clock Sunday Mass and I was giving this very heavy theological explanation of what I thought holiness and sanctity should be all about. It was a warm day and the windows of the church were open. All of a sudden in the window, on the left side of the church, appeared this great big fat gray cat. It just hopped up onto the windowsill and from the windowsill onto the head of the man sitting in the first pew; and then onto the pew and then onto the floor. The cat then proceeded to parade across the front of the church and then down the center aisle and out the main door of the church. Of course, everybody was in hysterics. I mean, really, it was funny. But as I said to the people then and I say it to you now, that cat was the holiest creature in the church at that moment, because that cat wasn't trying to be anything other than a cat. He was being true to what God created it to be. A beautiful creature being true to itself.

Christ is the model of holiness and Christ made man was fully human. He did not run away from life. He did not run away from people. He was always there and he didn't care who they were. He brought his presence to them. He knew his mission and he lived his mission. He accepted his suffering and he overcame his suffering. He could be joyful when it was time to be joyful and he could weep when it was time to weep and he knew the difference because he knew himself.

The key of holiness for anyone of us is to be ourselves. To be the person that God has created us to be. It means to be honest and real, to be truthful, to accept ourselves as human and not to fret over our humanness. Not to worry over our humanness but to rejoice in the fact that we are human with all that that implies, in spite of all the times we might stumble and fall. When we rejoice in the fact that we are human and when we are true to the person that God created us to be, then we are being holy. Then we are walking in holiness.. The word H.O.L.Y. simply means He Only Loves You.

Take Time for Reflection

Who are the saints (both living and dead) that surround your life?

What qualities make them faithful witnesses?

What encouragement do you draw from the saints in your life? From Jesus?

Do you consider yourself a saint?

I will work at being an effective witness of Jesus in everything I say and do.

16 Thanks

Now he who supplies seed to the sower and bread for food will also supply and increase your store of seed and will enlarge the harvest of your righteousness. You will be made rich in every way so that you can be generous on every occasion, and through us your generosity will result in thanksgiving to God. This service that you perform is not only supplying the needs of God's people but is also overflowing in many expressions of thanks to God. Because of the service by which you have proved yourselves, men will praise God for the obedience that accompanies your confession of the gospel of Christ, and for your generosity in sharing with them and with everyone else. And in their prayers for you their hearts will go out to you, because of the surpassing grace God has given you. Thanks be to God for his indescribable gift!

2 Corinthians 9:10-15

One time I came across this version of the Lord's Prayer that reflects the way that people without an awareness of God might pray.

Our brethren who are on earth, hallowed be our name.
Our kingdom come, our will be done on earth, for there is no heaven.
We must get this day our daily bread.
We neither forgive nor are forgiven.
We fear not temptation, for we deliver ourselves from evil.
Ours is the kingdom and the power, because there is no glory and no forever

How empty, how shallow, how self-serving this prayer is. Yet millions of Americans live their lives every day by following this philosophy. We enjoy a standard of living that is far beyond that experienced by people elsewhere in the world, yet we rarely pause to thank the Source of that abundance, the One who gives us life, breath, and all other blessings.

We will pray for God's help, but in the end we praise ourselves for finding the solutions to our problems. We will pray for healing, but praise medicine for the cure. Even the traditional *Grace* before meals tells God to bless us and the gifts we receive, but never mentions giving thanks to God for providing the meal.

We must never forget how blessed we are. We must always give thanks where it belongs.

> "Praise God from whom all blessings flow,
> Praise Him all creatures here below.
> Praise Him above ye heavenly host.
> Praise Father, Son, and Holy Ghost!"

Take Time for Reflection:

In saying that God made you rich, Paul is not just talking about money. What other things constitute riches?

In what ways has God made you rich?

What does "to say Grace" mean to you? When do you say Grace?

How can you thank God for His gift to you?

Today and every day of my life, I will praise God for all He has done for me by sharing the riches God has placed in my life.

17 Helping Hands

Come, you who are blessed by my Father; take your inheritance, the kingdom prepared for you since the creation of the world. For I was hungry and you gave me something to eat; I was thirsty and you gave me something to drink; I was a stranger and you invited me in; I needed clothes and you clothed me; I was sick and you looked after me; was in prison and you came to visit me. Then the righteous will answer him, "Lord when did we see you hungry and feed you, or thirsty and give you something to drink? When did we see you a stranger and invite you in, or needing clothes and clothe you? When did we see you sick or in prison and go to visit you? The King will reply, I tell you the truth, whatever you did for one of the least of these brothers of mine, that you did for me.
…He will reply, I tell you the truth, whatever you did not do for one of the least of these, you did not do for me.

Matthew 25:34-40, 45

For I was hungry and you gave me something to eat,

I am sure that there is a food center, which helps the hungry in your area,

What could I do to help them?

I was thirsty and you gave me something to drink,

We can thirst in many ways, most of us have water so freely that in our life I think thirst means something more…there are people in our lives who are thirsting to know the love of God—we are God's hands and feet, words and expression.

Who is thirsting for the peace, love and joy of Christ in my life?
I was a stranger and you invited me in,

So many people are so lonely, they need to be invited into my home or out to lunch or even for a phone conversation
I just thought of someone...

I needed clothes and you clothe me,

As Paul tells us in Colossians 3:12: Therefore, as God's chosen people, holy and dearly loved, clothe yourselves with compassion, kindness, humility, gentleness and patience. Who do I know, especially in my family and among my friends that need to be clothed this way?

Take Time for Reflection

Jesus taught us over and over that we as Christians were to care for those around us.
How have I taken this scripture quote into my heart?

Do I have a hard time giving only to family members and not to those around me?

Could I see myself examining my conscience using Jesus' criteria for entering the kingdom of Heaven?

What prevents me from reaching out to help others?

Based on this scripture quote I am going to formulate a personal project, one that I feel will fit my abilities and do something extra to help other people, people in my life that are not in my immediate family.

18 Speak My Language

> Ask and it will be given to you; seek and you will find; knock and the door will be opened to you. For everyone who asks receives; he who seeks finds; and to him who knocks, the door will be opened.
>
> Matthew 7:7-9

In London, years ago, there was an elephant named Bozo. He had been brought over from India and became a famous part of the circus. The children loved Bozo and he seemed to love the children. He would allow them to approach him and pet him. Often, he would take their little handfuls of peanuts and after gently sucking them up and twirling them into his mouth from his long trunk, he would almost seem to gesture thanks for their gift. Everyone just loved Bozo. He was the highlight of the circus. He was gentle, he was kind and he was loving.

Nobody really understood what happened to him but one day he changed. It was like he snapped. The trainer who brought in his breakfast every day was suddenly attacked. Bozo seemed to go after anyone who came near to him and he had to be secluded from the public. No one understood what happened but the reality was that he was no longer useful. He was no longer a ticket draw for the circus, and on top of it all, he was expensive to feed. He became quite a burden. The decision was made, Bozo would have to go and he would have to be replaced with another elephant. That would be expensive. A plan was formed. The circus would execute Bozo. They decided to advertise it as the demise of the mad elephant. They figured in order to recoup losses and maybe even make a profit to bring over another elephant from India they would sell tickets to see Bozo put down. They would put on an exhibit demonstrating Bozo behaving as a "mad elephant". Then they would have men come out in uniforms with their rifles and in unison shoot the elephant.

The ticket sale went on and before long they were sold out. The day of the execution the house would be packed. The circus would be making a handsome profit, so all was well that would end well. There was great excitement. Not only was every seat sold but also now they were even selling standing room only tickets. The curtain went up and the show began. Bozo was exhibiting all the qualities of a ferocious mad elephant and the crowd was in an uproar. Then came the moment of the execution. As the guns were drawn a small man from the audience jumped into the center of the ring. He went to the Ringmaster and asked him if he could spend time with the elephant. He felt that if he were allowed to be with Bozo for a short while he would be able to calm him and bring him back to his true nature of goodness. The crowd laughed and jeered but the man remained. The Ringmaster said to crowd, let's watch the show, figuring it would only add to everyone's enjoyment; but, before he allowed the man to approach the elephant he had him sign a waiver saying that if anything were to happen he would be released from responsibility. The little man took out a paper and pen and wrote that there would be no guilt assigned for whatever happened. Then he handed in the paper and approached the elephant. He began to crouch down and speak softly in a language that no one understood. At first Bozo began to roar but then he sort of cocked his head and he listened. The man kept speaking and then it was as if Bozo began to cry. He cried out loud first, then he whimpered and then he knelt down and rolled over onto his side. The crowd was in awe and the little man went over and patted him and kept talking. Bozo became tame and like his old self. When the man came out of the cage the Ringmaster walked over and asked the little man what it was that happened. He said, "I spoke to him in Indian, he is from India you know and he was just very homesick for his land. I believe if you hire a trainer that speaks Indian you will never have a problem again. He needs to hear that language. He is a good elephant."

Perhaps, we react the same as Bozo when we are misunderstood. Often we become frustrated and angry and lash out as Bozo did. When you are feeling that way, before you lash out try speaking it out to God. He speaks your language and he understands you. He is there for you...seek Him first.

Take Time for Reflection:

When you have a problem what steps do you take to resolve it?

How often to you look for God to give you the answer to your problems?

When we say we look to God for the solution how do we go about this?

Do we believe that if we ask God we will receive, when we seek we will find and if we knock he will open the door?

What seems to prevent that belief?

I will remind myself each day that God understands me, knows me and loves me. I will repeat this each morning and I will live my day with that thought making Him a real presence, that walks each minute with me, understands who I am and knows me inside and out.

19 Come On—Get In

If anyone would come after me, he must deny himself and take up his cross and follow me. For whoever wants to save his life will lose it, but whoever loses his life for me will find it. What good will it be for a man if he gains the whole world, yet forfeits his soul? Or what can a man give in exchange for his soul?

Matthew 16:27-27

Bobby was seven years old and very thrilled over the family vacation. His parents were both teachers and had saved their money and this year, they were going out West for the whole summer. They had arranged to spend time out on a ranch, helping with the chores and then having time to enjoy the animals. He was going to spend his whole summer living on a ranch and living like a cowboy. He was excited. The car was packed and off they were going.

They had arrived at the ranch and the next day was going to be the best! He found out when he got there that the Rodeo would be taking place right in the very town they were staying. There would be all different types of talent and contests exhibited. He went to bed that night but he just couldn't sleep. It was taking forever for morning to come. Then all of a sudden the sun was up and there was a knock on the door. "Come on Bobby" he heard his mother call. "It's time to get ready to go to the Rodeo if we want to get good seats."

Bobby bounded out of bed and before you know it he was sitting in the front row, you couldn't get a better seat than that. There was this contest and that taking place. One was more exciting than another was. Then there was a time out and entertainment began. There was a man who was riding on a tightrope back and forth with his bicycle. It was very exciting to watch, even scary as the man did not have a net under him to catch him. If he fell he was going to land in the bullpen and the bulls sure looked ready to get him. Bobby watched so intently. Before you knew the man looked down and called to Bobby. "Hey son, I am going to ride backwards over the rope this time, on a bike with a cart. Do you think it is possible that I can do this without falling into the pen?" "Yes!" Screamed Bobby, "I know you can." "Great, then come on—get in the cart and let's go!"

We all know that is an entirely different matter. We can be like that with God. So much of what we are saying is "lip service". We say we know He is sovereign, we know He rules the earth, but we don't live like that. We spend too much time worrying and stressed out. Keep your focus on Jesus and you will find peace, you will know He is with you in all things and there is nothing that you and He can't handle together.

Take Time for Reflection:

What do you think it means by denying yourself?

What do you think prevents you from surrendering to God's will?

On the other hand, what has helped you to make that surrender?

Do I believe that God has a definite plan for my life?

There are many things in my life that are causing me stress and keep me from the peace of living in the Lord. I will take a look at what has me running and going and doing. When my life is not part of God's plan I do not have that inner peace. Things around can be stressful but walking with God is what gives me peace. I will look at my life and see what it is that's preventing me from being one with the Lord.

20 The Painting

Therefore, as God's chosen people, holy and dearly loved, clothe yourselves with compassion, kindness, humility, gentleness and patience. Bear with each other and forgive whatever grievances you may have against one another. Forgive as the Lord forgave you. And over all these virtues put on love, which binds them all together in perfect unity. Let the peace of Christ rule in your hearts, since as members of one body you were called to peace. And be thankful. Let the word of Christ dwell in you richly as you teach and admonish one another with all wisdom, and as you sing psalms, hymns and spiritual songs with gratitude in your hearts to God. And whatever you do, whether in word or deed, do it all in the name of the Lord Jesus, giving thanks to God the Father through him.

Col 3:12-17

One evening, a group of ministry workers were having dinner at the home of a woman prior to a service. The woman was a widow, about eighty years old. During the meal, someone noticed a picture of a young, smiling Jesus hanging on the dining room wall. We all commented on the beauty of the portrait and asked where she had gotten it.

She responded that she didn't want to bore us with a long explanation, but since we asked, she'd tell us.

It seems that the woman's grandson has lived with her and her husband during the years he was growing up. Often, he would take her bible and look at the prayer cards and pictures she kept in it. One of the cards had a drawing of a young Jesus. She always commented that this was her favorite picture of the Lord.

When the grandson turned eighteen, he moved to another state to find work. Five years later, when the young man was visiting the grandmother around the holidays, he took the card from her bible and had an artist do a portrait from it. On Christmas Eve, he presented the woman with the painting. The following day, the young man was killed in an automobile accident.

Hearing this, all of us in the room felt a great rush of sympathy for the woman. Our feeling was that she must experience great pain when she looked at the painting. But the opposite was true. Her comment was that whenever she looked at the picture of Jesus, she thanked God for giving her a grandson for twenty-three years.

The woman really had the peace of Christ dwelling in her heart. She learned, as we all should, to look at the positive side of every happening. She also showed us that being thankful to God is the real key to that peace

Take Time for Reflection:

How can we clothe ourselves with the virtues?

How can we find the peace of Christ? What attitudes must we develop to find that peace?

What part does prayer and scripture play in finding peace?

I will continuously work on developing a positive attitude of thanksgiving. I will focus on the positives rather than the negatives in my life.

21 One Thing Leads to Another

He also said, "This is what the kingdom of God is like. A man scatters seed on the ground. Night and day, whether he sleeps or gets up, the seed sprouts and grows; though he does not know how. All by itself the soil produces grain-first the stalk, then the head, then the full kernel in the head. As soon as the grain is ripe, he puts the sickle to it, because the harvest has come."

Mark 4:26-30

Olympic athletes realize that the first step in the race is as important as the last. One thing builds on another. Each practice, day by day, makes it possible to one-day dream of being in the world stadium, putting on the gold—winning first place. The preparation for that event takes place daily. It is impossible to practice once in a while and be a winner. It is the same with life...it is the day by day decisions that determine our outcome. We know this in an athletic competition, but it works the same in day today living. One thing builds onto the next. Where it is even better for us is that aside from performing true and kind acts each day if we surrender to God our lives He will be working while we aren't even aware.

God has built inside of each of us a potential for strength. "Night and day, whether he sleeps or gets up, the seed sprouts and grows, though he does not know how" (Mark 4). We can if we surrender, connect to this power. Each decision of our day should be to make everything and everyone we touch a little bit better...including our own selves. God is living in each present moment of our life, amazing. He is working while we sleep; our very breath is a sign of that.

When I was very young and in kindergarten, I was taught a very simple but powerful prayer. It was the morning offering and it simply said,

> *"Oh God I offer up this day all I shall think, do and say, uniting it with what was done on earth by Jesus Christ your Son."*

The prayer is so simple and yet so powerful. It surrenders the thoughts the actions and the words of the day and puts them into the control of God. It is a day by day exercise, one thing building on to another for a fulfilled and peaceful life

Take Time for Reflection:

In this scripture Jesus is telling us that invisible forces are at work, the Kingdom of God is present and around you…do you realize that?

Right now as we are closing in on the end of the millennium people are saying, "Jesus will come again, the end of the world is quickly approaching". What do you feel about that?

Do you find yourself being impatient for justice and asking, "When will corruption end?"

The growth of the seed is cumulative; day by day it changes and takes shape depending on the things around it. Do we realize that day by day our growth with the Lord is cumulative, depending on our decisions?

How do we go about nourishing the roots of our life, while we are waiting for the harvest to come?

:

I will trust the Lord to help me make the decisions necessary in my life to bring me into a closer relationship with God. I will trust that he will be at work, morning and night helping me to be in a close relationship with him since this is his will. Each day that I will remember his presence and rely on it

22 A Light

You are the light of the world. A city built on a hilltop cannot be hidden. No one lights a lamp to put it under a tub; they put it on the lamp-stand where it shines for everyone in the house. In the same way your light must shine in the sight of men, so that, seeing your good works, they may give the praise to your Father in heaven.

Matthew 5:14-17

The woman was in the 7-Eleven Store and she appeared so upset. She kept walking outside, wringing her hands and looking up and down the road. Whatever could be her problem? I had just arrived with my husband to buy some cups of coffee, and while he was in the shop I sat in the car and observed the woman. She then walked back in and spoke with the store manager. I saw him pick up the phone, dial and wait a few minutes. Then he looked back at the woman and shook his head "No," and proceeded to wait on other customers. The woman's distress was growing and growing. With that my husband left the store and got in the car. He hadn't noticed anything while he was in there but I asked him to wait and watch the woman and see what he thought. After a few minutes, with her leaving the store once again, standing out front, looking up and down and then walking back in he felt the same way I did. Something was wrong; the poor woman's anxiety level was increasing and increasing.

I said I think I should offer help to this person but I feel strange. I hope that she won't think that I am a problem and just add on to her anxiety. But, I took a deep breath and decided that I would take the risk. I went into the shop and explained that I had been sitting outside and saw that something was wrong and that I was wondering if I could help. She looked at me and started to cry. She had taken the bus to go home but had fallen asleep and slept past her stop. She didn't know what to do to get home and every time she placed a call her family did not answer. She was low on cash and did not have enough money for a taxi. I offered her a ride and she gratefully accepted. It was right on our way and it only took about five minutes to have her deposited by her home. It was such an easy way to lend a hand. I was so glad I offered.

Shortly after that happened I was in church and the priest spoke about acting quicker to do God's work. He said we often hesitate and become shy to reach out and do a good. We feel that we will be embarrassed or that it will not be accepted or that we will appear strange. He told us to act quickly when a "good" idea comes into mind for that could be, and most likely is, the prompting of the Holy Spirit. He pointed out that the Spirit could not act without our help! He pointed out how quickly we react to Satan's prompting when we get angry, usually we just fly off the handle and speak harshly to one another. He said we must learn to stop there and react quickly for Christ! How true that statement is!

Take Time for Reflection:

What sort of things could I do that would bring glory to the Father and not myself?

You have heard of the term, "emptying yourself and putting on Christ." Have you experienced such a feeling in your life, when?

What were the results of that experience?

What means do you use to be the "Light of the World"?

Go forward, turn on your heart lights and touch those you meet each day even if it is only with a smile!

Prayer of Cardinal Newman

Dear Lord, help me to spread your fragrance wherever I go. Flood my soul with your spirit and life. Penetrate and possess my whole being so utterly that all my life may only be a radiance of yours.

Shine through me, and be so in me that every soul I come in contact with may feel your presence in my soul. Let them look up and see no longer me, but only you Oh Lord! Stay with me, then I shall begin to shine as you do, so to shine as to be a light to others. The light Oh Lord will be all from you, none of it will be mine; it will be you shinning on others through me. Let me thus praise you in the way you love best, by shining on those around me.

Let me preach you without preaching, not by words but by my example, by the catching force, the sympathetic influence of what I do the evident fullness of the love my heart bears to you. Amen

23 Humility - Self Esteem

> Your attitude should be the same as that of Christ Jesus: Who, being in very nature God, did not consider equality with God something to be grasped, but made himself nothing, taking the very nature of a servant, being made in human likeness. And being found in appearance as a man, he humbled himself and became obedient to death-- even death on a cross! Therefore God exalted him to the highest place and gave him the name that is above every name, that at the name of Jesus every knee should bow, in heaven and on earth and under the earth, and every tongue confess that Jesus Christ is Lord, to the glory of God the Father.
>
> Philippians 2:5-11

When you partner together, humility and self-esteem, so often we get confused and think that one would contradict the other. But no, they go hand in hand for the truth is we must see our worth in that fact that God loves us. He loves us individually as He loves no one else and no one more. He created us and He shines His love down on us constantly. All we are able to do receive a gift and a blessing from Him. It is as simple as this: right down to each and every breath that we take is His gift. His love makes us so worthy—worth more than millions of treasures.

Each thing that I call mine—the things that make up my person is a gift from God. I determine how I will take care of that gift or how I will ignore that gift. My hair, will I comb it, curl it etc. My nails, will I bite them or let them grow, my body, will I eat properly or will I eat without benefit. Everything I do is a decision on how to use the gifts that God has given to me. It is as simple and as complicated as that. He has given me dominion over these things. How I use these gifts is my choice. I can cherish and take care of what He has given or I can destroy. It is up to me. When I realize this, I realize that each thing I do is a decision...that is enough to comprehend isn't it?

It is amazing when this reality comes home. We often feel that we were born, given a name and we grow. We act and make decisions and our life takes twists and turns. We think we are the one in control because He has given us the gift of free will. We do determine the outcome of things and then we get confused. We forget that God is our supplier, the force. It is He who makes us breathe and who created us with the ability to accomplish everything. Our gift to God can only be our "Yes". That is all we have to give Him.

After our "Yes", the surrender that we put off for so long and were so frightened of has not put us in touch with His plan, we begin to stretch, to reach out and to do more and then we ever thought that we could; we see His grace. We go beyond our capabilities to do His will and we realize that we have connected to a power, then we learn the truth: that we are nothing without Him and In Him, Through Him and With Him we can do unbelievable things.

In our walk with God we must learn to hold on to things loosely. If we hold on to what He has given us too tightly and do not let go we will not have room for the next gift that He is sending. Your Father will always give to you, He has been giving to you all the time, even when you didn't notice. He has new things in store for you always. Always know that He challenges, and brings on new horizons. He cannot keep giving if you don't accept.

Lord I realize how much you have done and I realize that I am probably not even aware of the numerous times you have helped me. Lord, I want to grow in awareness of your love for me. Your Love has filled me with self-esteem.

Take Time for Reflection:

List the blessings that you have received from God.

Do a litany of Thanksgiving for these gifts: I thank you Lord for........., Thank you Lord

Can you picture yourself "connected" to God?

Think and in your heart, what is it that you could give to God?

Remember a time when you felt God's grace in your life.

I will concentrate on the things that God has done in my life. I will pay special attention to that, I will call up His presence at different times in my day and I will begin to get in touch with His love for me. I will keep thinking on His love for me, me as an individual, me as his friend, brother, sister, spouse. With Him, In Him, Through Him will be my prayer.

24 That All May Be One

As you sent me into the world, I have sent them into the world. For them I sanctify myself, that they too may be truly sanctified. My prayer is not for them alone. I pray also for those who will believe in me through their message, that all of them may be one, Father, just as you are in me and I am in you. May they also be in us so that the world may believe that you have sent me. I have given them the glory that you gave me, that they may be one as we are one: I in them and you in me. May they be brought to complete unity to let the world know that you sent me and have loved them even as you have loved me. Father, I want those you have given me to be with me where I am, and to see my glory, the glory you have given me because you loved me before the creation of the world. Righteous Father, though the world does not know you, I know you, and they know that you have sent me. I have made you known to them, and will continue to make you known in order that the love you have for me may be in them and that I myself may be in them.

John 17:18-26

In the Gospel of John, the Last Supper concludes with Jesus addressing the disciples one last time. He reminds them of God's faithful love and promises them a share in the unity he experiences with the Father. By virtue of our baptism we too have a share in God's very own life. We also have a responsibility to foster that unity by sharing His life with others.

I remember hearing a story about Jesus: that went something like this
Jesus Christ said he had never been to a football match. So we took him to one, my friends and I. It was a ferocious battle between the Protestant Punchers and the Catholic Crusaders. The Crusaders scored first; Jesus cheered wildly and threw his hat high up into the air. Then the Punchers scored. And Jesus cheered wildly and again threw his hat into the air.

This seemed to puzzle the man behind us. He tapped Jesus on the shoulder and asked, "Which side are you shouting for, my good man?" "Me?" replied Jesus, by now visibly excited by the game. "Oh! I'm not shouting for either side. I'm just here to enjoy the game." The questioner turned to his neighbor and sneered, "Hmmm, an atheist,"

On the way back we briefed Jesus on the religious situation of the world today. "It's funny about religious people, Lord," we said. "They always seem to think that God is only on their side and against the people on the other." Jesus agreed, "That is why I don't back religions. I back people," he said, "People are more important than religions. Man is more important than the Sabbath."

"You ought to watch your words," one of us said with some concern. "You were crucified once for saying that sort of thing, you know." "Yes, and by religious people," said Jesus with a wry smile.

There is no room in our lives for judgmental attitudes. Mutual respect and tolerance are the only hallmarks that can mark a Christian. This is the only way we can help answer Jesus' prayer "that all may be one."

Take Time for Reflection:

When has someone's love for you been an experience of God's love?

How does living in God's love bring you joy?

What steps can you take to insure that "all may be one"?

I will live in the Love of God by sharing His love with everyone I meet. I will work toward unity by treating others as if they were Christ, himself, remembering his words: "Do not judge, or you too will be judged."

Matthew 7:1

25 Having an Anxiety Attack?

As Jesus and His disciples were on their way, he came to a village where a woman named Martha opened her home to him. She had a sister called Mary, who sat at the Lord's feet listening to what he said. But Martha was distracted by all the preparations that had to be made. She came to him and asked, "Lord, don't you care that my sister has left me to do the work by myself. Tell her to help me! " "Martha, Martha," the Lord answered, "You are worried and upset about many things, but only one thing is needed. Mary has chosen what is better and it will not be taken away from her."

Luke 10:38-43

The day Jesus dropped in on Mary and Martha I am sure he was tired and glad for the rest. Jesus, like us, needed a place to relax and to just be with people and enjoy their company. Unfortunately, Martha knew she was the hostess and desiring to be the hostess with the "moistest" she just couldn't relax. Can you picture how annoyed she was getting in that kitchen? It must have been working on her for a long time before she finally exploded. I am sure she just couldn't believe that Jesus would not take her side. She probably thought that he would sympathize with her and tell Mary to go to the kitchen and help. She must have been shocked when he said, "Oh Martha, Martha"…you have it all wrong! Sometimes when I get myself all worked up over something, I am sure I would do well to take a second look. Possibly, there could be a better way. Mary's faith won over Martha's panic!

Did you ever hear the story of the king who died and the family was left to make all the preparations for the funeral? Well, as it was told the prince and his wife and servants worked day and night so that the funeral would be just perfect. Relatives and friends from far and wide began to come to pay their respects. So many visitors came that the task of attending to their needs became tremendously difficult. The prince and his wife and family began to chip in to help the staff with their chores so that each guest would be comfortable. The elaborate funeral was planned but the night before it was to take place the weary prince begged the people to return to their homes just for that evening and give them a chance to rest. The next day the king was buried and the people were invited to the lavish feast. Those who went were wined and dined but there were many who refused to go because the prince had not entertained them the night before. They felt that he had been rude to them. The prince put out a decree referring to this tiresome group as "Bad, Odd and Offensive Relative"...thus the term BOOR came into existence.

The moral of the story is: You should always try to be a prince, but don't let the boors get you down!

Take Time for Reflection:

How often do we find ourselves too busy to take the time to talk and to listen to someone we love?

Do we find ourselves too busy to even recognize the presence of God in our life?

Can we find Jesus in our work or do we find ourselves accomplishing many things only to be finished and feeling empty?

 Do we find ourselves even fretting in our prayer life, listing our needs over and over? Do we take time to sit quiet and "listen" to His will in our life?

So often I find myself running to do this or that and really just going in circles. I will make an effort to meditate, using my Christian beliefs to put myself at peace, sitting quietly, calling on the presence of God. I will take the time to be still, whether it is by taking a walk, sitting before the Blessed Sacrament, finding someway to be alone concentrating on the presence of God in my life. I will find a way to relax with the Lord.

26 The Choice

Rejoice in the Lord always. I say it again, rejoice and may everyone experience your gentle and understanding heart. The Lord is near; do not be anxious about anything. In everything resort to prayer and supplications together with thanksgiving and bring your requests before God. Then the peace of God, which surpasses all understanding, will keep your hearts and minds in Christ Jesus.

Philippians 4:4-5

God I am feeling so desperate. Things just don't seem to be working out at all. Are you there? I feel so alone. Could there be a lonelier feeling than when we are facing a situation not knowing where to turn to get relief. So often it seems like money could fix anything. Even when it comes to illness if I only had the funds to travel here or there for this or that medical treatment. Fear grows, the feeling of abandonment moves in when times get tough like this. No matter how many times in the past God's help has been clearly perceived the present moment seems to indicate that he is not noticing this time. This time the situation has slipped through the cracks and God just isn't aware or isn't concerned.

I don't really believe that. I know, especially, when it comes to everyone else's problem I have the answer. I have such strong faith...I am always saying, don't worry God has a plan for your life. He is there, He never abandons us, but when it is late at night, and I have gone over and over the situation I begin to wonder is he hearing me? Does he care? Everyone who has been in this situation knows this feeling of anxiety. Day passes onto day and we panic. We begin to count on anything but God to help us. That is when we get into trouble.

It is at this time that we have to put the brakes on and stop the negative thinking. It is like being on a roller coaster and you don't have to ride the car all the way into the ground. You say you can't seem to control the thoughts. Certainly you can. Think of the times you were so angry and then the phone rang and in the middle of your anger you sweetly say "Hello" into the receiver. All of a sudden you were in control of your emotions. You can still do that. Make the choice. Don't lean on anything else to support you. Take a positive approach and turn to God. Take out the Bible, open it and read. The words are comforting and true. The words show that people have had the same problems, more or less throughout history. Jesus tells us not to worry, that the Father is Abba and he loves us so much. We are not forgotten. All of a sudden, and usually on the day we least expect it, his answer comes. Most often our prayer is answered in a surprising way, a way we hadn't even imagined. God is faithful. As Paul reminds us: "All things work for the good for those who love him." Romans 8:28

Remember: He is your God—and he calls you a beloved child.

Take Time for Reflection:

How do we handle our problems?

Our problems in the past give rise to our faith in the present moment?

How can our problems be a faith builder for others?

It is even a witness to share fears and doubts. Can we be free enough to do that?

Explain what is meant by the "Peace that surpasses all understanding."

When I am fearful I will remember and pray the words in Philippians: "The Lord is near; do not be anxious about anything. In everything resort to prayer..." I will say this over and over until the situation passes, for I know the choice—stay in the Lord and peace will follow.

27 Make God #1

You shall have no other gods before me.

Deuteronomy 5:7

What does it mean to have a god? A god is something that we expect good things from, something we have learned to count on, to trust in, and to look towards for protection. Simply stated to have a god is to have something we trust and we believe. Know that in all reality your god is that which you give your heart and on which you place confidence.

Is that in money? Is that in health? Is that in friendship? What do I consider "top priority" in my life? Whatever it is, it is pulling your focus away from truth, that is, that God is your creator and He alone should be the priority.

Do you remember a segment in the Art Linkletter Show, called "Kids Say the Darndest Things?" Well, one afternoon I remember talking with a little guy named Tim. He was about four years old at the time and was really happy about a superman sticker he had gotten for Christmas. He had wanted that sticker for the longest time and finally he was able to get one and put it on his bike. Proud as could be he left the house to peddle around the neighborhood and show his friends. Well, things didn't go quite as Tim had planned and it seemed that the kids on the block thought the sticker was pretty dumb and made fun of Tim for having it. There he was back home trying with all his might to get the sticker off the bike. I remember saying to him that he would just have to learn in life to ignore things like that and go forward with what he wanted to do. After a few minutes I remember Tim saying, "What does ignore mean?" I told him it meant not paying attention to what other people were saying. Almost immediately Tim looked up and said, "I don't think that we should ignore Jesus, do you?" Surprised I asked him what ever made him say that, because I agree I don't think we should ignore Jesus either. Then Tim said, "why everybody sings that every Christmas, 'Oh come let us ignore Him'." That sounds so cute but even at the time of Christmas which is dedicated to the birth of Christ we get so caught up in the gift giving, the entertaining and decorating that we probably do appear to be ignoring Him. Let's make sure that we are living each day with the idea of "Come Let Us Adore Him."

Once a businessman was asked the question, "What is your occupation?" The businessman answered, "I am a Christian." The man was then asked, "What is your job?" The businessman replied, "I am a Christian." "No, no said the other person, you don't understand, I am trying to find out what it is you do for a living?' Oh that's a different story said the businessman, "My full time job is to be a Christian; however, I also own a Seven Eleven Store to pay the bills".

Make God number one in your life.

Take Time For Reflection:

What is it that is taking up all my time and my energy?

At the beginning of the day, when I leave my home, what am I trying to accomplish, what god am I really serving?

Do I search out the god of money, power, lust, popularity?

What is it that really concerns me? What am I afraid to lose?

What do I have to do to set my priorities in order?

What should I get rid of in my life that is pulling me away from God?

I will make it a point to begin my day more aware of where I will spend my time and my energy. I will ask God to give me the grace to say and mean, *"All for you Dear God, All for you."*

NOTES

NOTES

Made in the USA
Middletown, DE
25 June 2015